SINGLE AGAIN

SINGLE *Again*

LIVING ALONE AND LIKING IT

Anita Naik

Illustration by Susan Hellard

Piccadilly Press · London

Phototypeset by Goodfellow & Egan, Cambridge,
Printed and bound by Biddles, Guildford,
for the publishers, Piccadilly Press Ltd.,
5 Castle Road, London NW1 8PR
A catalogue record for this book is available
from the British Library
ISBN 1-85340-143-9 (hardback)
ISBN 1-85340-148-X (trade paperback)

Anita Naik lives in South London. She started out as a staff writer for *Just Seventeen* and then became its Agony Aunt. She is now a freelance journalist for *More*, *Smash Hits*, and the *Guardian*. She is currently working on a programme for Channel 4. This is her first book.

Susan Hellard lives in North London. She is a very popular illustrator who has worked extensively in both advertising and publishing. She has illustrated many books for Piccadilly Press.

Contents

ACKNOWLEDGEMENTS
With grateful thanks to Jenni Baxter and Fiona Robertson for their encouragement and help and also to all my other friends who make being single or not, a laugh a minute.

"Courage consists not of the absence of fear, but of the capacity to move ahead even though one is afraid."
Rollo May

INTRODUCTION

Your worst nightmare's come true – you're single again! Destined once more to spend your nights alone with only a box of chocolates and a packet of Kleenex for company. But STOP! Before you go any further, think! There was life before him and there's definitely a life after him.

Of course, I know from my own experience, suddenly becoming a single woman again can make you feel like a visitor from Mars. People look at you strangely, treat you differently and, worse still, vary between a pitying and condescending attitude towards you. The one thing they don't do is leave you alone. It's almost as if, in becoming single again, you've become a social misfit.

Just check out the bookshops, see if you can find a book called Smart Men, Foolish Choices or anything of that ilk. Instead there's a steady stream of books just waiting to tell you how and why women are going wrong in the name of love. This, thankfully, isn't one of those books!

I don't know why relationships don't always work and nor does anyone else. If someone did, you could bet your last penny that they'd be out there right now, declaring a miracle, marketing it like crazy and selling it left, right and centre.

Instead there's one truth about becoming single – it isn't the end of the world. Of course, it's a sad fact in our society that single men are more acceptable than single women. Men seem to be able to perfect the little-boy-lost routine so well, that even the most ardent feminist could well find herself trying to help them out. Single women, on the other hand, are looked upon slightly suspiciously. People can't wait to say, "Hello, got a boyfriend yet?" or more disturbingly, "Well, I suppose you're a career woman aren't you?" Others feel threatened by our presence and think, "What's wrong with her? Why's she single?" Mix this with our own fears about being lonely in old age and always being the odd one out and it's no wonder some of us are browbeaten into thinking we have to find a man again fast.

So why not turn things around? Women are supposed to be happier being single. Look at your single friends – some, especially those who aren't newly single or have always been single, are for the most part, happy.

If you choose to enjoy your new single status, you will improve your life beyond measure. All it takes is courage and determination.

Chapter One

GOING SOLO

1. Being Single – The Bad and the Good

Part of the trouble with being single again is being faced with a world full of couples. Most adverts seem destined to reiterate this point, whether they're for cars, coffee or razor blades; they are all geared towards couples living it up in the bliss of togetherness. Magazines and films are always declaring the wonders of a life together. Even supermarkets manage to get in on the act and are notorious for rarely making portions small enough for one, which means you end up with either a food mountain to match the EC's or nights chomping endless pasta dishes. Even friends' dinner parties, where you are conveniently (but always embarrassingly) placed next to the last single man, become a journey into hell. And the worst peril of being single again, is the way your best friend turns into a parody of Cilla Black on "Blind Date" – always trying to find you that perfect date and mate!

What is constantly overlooked is that almost all of us at some point in our life, will be single. Whether it's because of a break-up, a divorce, bereavement or just because we choose to be, the fact is we are on our own. This book isn't addressing how you came to be single but concerns itself with how to live happily being single.

"I didn't feel that bad about breaking up with my boyfriend and being single again, till the people around started in on me. They kept saying, you're brave to attempt life on your own. As if I was about to climb Mount Everest or something! The thing is, I knew they were calling me a fool behind my back, and

secretly worrying if I was going to become an embarrassing burden to them."
Anna (30)

"I know I shouldn't feel ashamed about being single but somehow I can't help feeling a failure about it. It's almost as if I take it as a sign that I'm not attractive or clever enough to have a boyfriend."
Sue (45)

Ask yourself what is *so bad* about being single? So what if you haven't got a boyfriend to cuddle up to? It doesn't mean that you are unattractive or stupid. Look at all the famous and glamorous women who manage to flourish on their own: Madonna, Cher, Juliet Stevenson, Glenda Jackson, Mary Wesley, Kate Adie and Shirley McLaine to name but a few. Sure, they're in and out of relationships, but they're more successful in their own right and as single women, than as part of a couple.

In this life you cannot rely on someone else to make you either complete or happy. Happiness is something that you have to work at by yourself. If you rely on a boyfriend/husband to fulfil you or to provide a meaning in your life you lay yourself open to total desolation when they are gone. In order to become a happy person you have to become complete on your own. This means relying on yourself to be happy whether you are single/married or living with someone.

"At first, all I could see was the downside of being single, no company, being alone, getting fat because there was nothing to do but eat. But I was wrong. When I really thought about it, I realised that this was the first time in my life that I was free to do whatever I wanted. Now, I do more with my life than I did when I was living with my boyfriend."
Crysta (25)

REJECT SHOP

2. It's Not So Great Being a Couple

How many people do you know, who are miserable within a relationship? One, four, ten . . . all your friends? How many times have you heard them lament, "We fight all the time but it's better than being on my own." The sad truth of the matter is that many people would rather stay in an unsatisfactory relationship than have no relationship. Think about your last one; no doubt there were times when you spent lonely moments in the company of your partner and yet, many people still feel that loneliness on their own is worse than loneliness with someone else. The truth is, loneliness is loneliness whichever way you look at it.

"When I met Gary, I loved him so much because he was so full of energy. We filled our days completely, always seeing friends, going out etc. When he left me I felt like he'd taken my life with him. Suddenly I had no-one around to provide entertainment and fill my days for me. It was such a shock. It was only when I started doing things for myself did I realise that I had hated most of the things we used to do together.
Frances (24)

There are also negative points to being in a relationship. So, next time you're feeling down, remember the good things about being single:
(1) You've still got friends to lean on, and people that care.
(2) You can look after yourself rather than him.
(3) You can look at, talk to, and even flirt with other men without worrying that someone will be jealous or kick up a fuss.
(4) You are a free spirit. This means you can develop your personality any way you please. Plus, you can choose when to go out, who to go out with and when to leave.
(5) You no longer have to compromise over a single thing.

No longer will you be carted along to the cinema on a Saturday night to see Revenge of The Killer Zombies IV, when you really wanted to watch something you could weep unashamedly over.
(6) There is no need to ask permission for anything.
(7) You have no worries about spending time with your friends and then being accused of neglect.
(8) You no longer have to cook meals that you hate and, better still, you can eat when *you* want to.

"The best part about being single is putting the key in the door and knowing I won't have to face another accusation or another, 'Why haven't you . . .'"
Jo (30)

Doctors now say that women living on their own show fewer stress symptoms than couples living together. The result of this is that single women live longer and healthier lives.

"I used to get terrible nervous rashes and headaches when I was married. I never knew why I got them till I got divorced. I used to think it was having kids or an allergy to something. It was only later that I realised it came from the stress of my marriage.
Mary (40)

Being on your own is something you should make the most of. Allow being single to widen your horizons and let you become your own person. There is no security in looking backwards, and lamenting over a lost relationship. Once something is finished, accepting it's over is the first step to recovery. No amount of pining or wishing is going to make your relationship return. So, for once, concentrate on the future. In time, if you want another relationship it will come along, but a knight in shining armour rescuing you from your single life isn't likely to happen. Being content with your own company and space is a sure way to become attractive to the opposite sex. After all, everyone loves someone who loves herself.

3. Being Single – The Statistics

Even though more and more people are leading lives on their own, single people are seen as being a minority and therefore, slightly odd. The truth is according to the 1990 census, there are a total of 12 million adults living in England and Wales who are not married at the present moment. Twelve million people who live their lives either single or in and out of relationships. Luckily, singles break down into different categories, and ones that thankfully break away from the everyday view of who and what singles should be. Think about these statistics: two million people in the 45 to 64 year age range are single but only a quarter of them have been widowed, compared to a third who have never been married. While in the 25 to 44-year-old age group, four million people have not yet been married. Staggering statistics, when you compare it to the fact that the average age for a woman to get married in this country is 23 years old.

With all these single people living, working and breathing you'd think other people would start to take more note of them. Not that the singles are being totally ignored. You only have to pick up a listings magazine to see the lonely hearts columns reach back over at least four pages. Then there's the rise of game shows like "Blind Date" and dating

agencies whose main aim seems to be to show that single women are only after one thing – a boyfriend! Little of the industry surrounding singles even considers for one moment that single people are happy too.

"It was the fear that somehow I'd be alone when I became single that held me back for years. I kept looking at all my friends and thinking, 'My God, I really am the last single female on this planet.' It also seemed to me that every remotely desirable man was attached. It was only when I widened my circle of friends and started mixing with different people with different interests that I realised how wrong I'd been."
Claire (34)

Despite the common view that single women outnumber single men, there are equal numbers of single men and women in this country. Take heart, among the 12 million unmarried people out there, there are plenty who feel just like you.

The problem with not being able to find them, lies with the way we pick our friends. Think about what you were like at 16 years old. The chances are you knew lots of different people from lots of different backgrounds. As we grow older and become part of a couple, we naturally mix with people who have similar lives to our own. Obviously, when we change our circumstances, we view our friends in a different light. Suddenly we become aware of how nicely paired off everyone is and how much we stick out.

"I love my friends, they've been brilliant but they seem to be on a mission to pair me up with any passing male. The other day, one of them even commented that her postman was single! They seem so desperate to relieve me of my newly found freedom, that they keep saying hardly anyone's single – as if I should be ashamed of my status."
Sian (37)

What do these statistics ultimately mean to you and me? Well, hopefully, they'll convince any misguided single person out there that they are definitely not alone in the world.

4. Overcoming the Fear of Freedom

What does the word 'free' mean to you? Does it lighten your heart? Does it conjure up images of birds flying with reckless abandon in blue skies? Perhaps it feels more like a cold and lonely jail cell. If the latter is true, you're not alone. Many people fear freedom, imagining it to be some desert island. In their minds the thought of actually going out there and dealing with it, strikes terror so pure in their hearts that they'd rather be unhappy than give it a try.

Yet learning to deal with being single is rather like starting a new relationship, it's just a different state of affairs. You have to go through the same process of educating yourself to deal with it, cope with it, have fun with it and ultimately live with it. You have to teach yourself to cope with problems as they arise and not conquer everything in one day.

The first and most important step to getting there is learning to look at your life from a different perspective.

Take the story of two identical twins. One is a pessimist, the other an optimist. As part of an experiment the pessimist is placed in a room laden with riches, expensive clothes and lots of food. The optimist is left in a room full of horse manure. A day later the pessimist is led out. She is miserable and bored.

"What's wrong?" asks the psychologist.

"There was no-one to keep me company. I didn't want to ruin the clothes and I didn't eat anything because I didn't want to put on weight," she replied.

The door to the optimist's room was opened and there she sat happy and contented.

"Why are you so happy?" asked the psychologist.

"Well," she replied, "with all this horse shit there must be a pony."

The point of this tale is to show that the same situation

can look good or bad depending on which way you choose to view it.

"I used to think being on my own was so terrible for my kids. I'd look at them and think – poor things, they've only got one parent to love them and look after them. Then one day my daughter said, 'I'm glad we've only got you mum because it means we only get shouted at once when we're being awful.' That made me laugh and see that things really aren't that bad."
Sue (34)

How to Get a New Perspective

(1) Choose to be positive and every morning when you wake up, instead of thinking, "Oh no! Another day by myself," think, "I'm my own person, I can go where I want, do what I want and be whoever I want to be." This is the joy of being single and on your own. Freedom is a gift in life, one that should be treasured not fought. It doesn't have to mean loneliness, despair and futility.
(2) Think of your new life as being free from strings. There's no-one around to ask where you're going, who you're going with and why you're late. Freedom means time for yourself, even if you choose to use this time to read or daydream, it's your time.

"When I was married to Keith I used to blame the kids for me not having any time. But it was only when I was divorced that I realised it wasn't them at all. I used to purposely keep myself busy because Keith made me feel guilty about wasting my time just reading or sitting down. Now my spare time is bliss."
Debbie (32)

(3) Think of all the experimenting and growing that freedom allows you to enjoy. Realise that at any age it's never too late to change your life and make it what you want it to be. Freedom can bring happiness as long as you let it.

Chapter Two

LONELINESS

1. Painful Memories

We all use memories as an escape route when things get bad. How many times have you got through a terrible night out by remembering the good times? Memories are a safety valve for when times get just too awful. Yet it doesn't take much to let them get out of hand and take control of your present. And no-one wants to end up like Miss Haversham from Dickens's *Great Expectations*, still dressed in her faded wedding dress, reliving her past instead of living for herself.

Memories always hit you like a lead weight when you're least expecting them. Picture the scene, there you are happily clearing out your bag, when lo and behold you find some old ticket stubs to that concert you went to last summer. So what if you hated it, the car broke down and you argued all the way through it, it still reminds you of "him" and just when you think you're over him this occurs and BANG! you're right back there at step one, lonely, miserable and full of memories.

"Every time I turned on the radio I'd hear a song that would remind me of the times we had together. It didn't really matter what the song was, something within it would trigger off a memory in my mind. Once my friends were horror struck when I burst into tears after hearing a bit of the Birdie Song. It wasn't our song or anything, it actually reminded me of the time we were at a wedding together!"
Lorna (28)

During the early stages of being single, trying to break ties with the past is hard but you can do it.
(1)Decide to get over him. We know that disengaging your thoughts and habits from someone else's, especially when you've been together for a long time, is hard, but for your own peace of mind you have to decide to do it.

"At first I would spend hours dissecting what had happened to our relationship. Thinking if only I had done this or that, things would have worked out. The positive thing it did was help me clear my head but negatively it just made me think about the break-up all the time. Then, one day I heard a girl at work say I was a sad woman, spending my life living through past memories. She made me feel like a completely useless and pathetic person. After that I made sure I never talked about what had happened in public again. I'm sure this is why it's taken me so long to get over things."
Claire (34)

"It took me a long time to get over Steve. I kept saying I was over him and our relationship hadn't mattered that much to me. The truth is, it had. It was only when I kept on coming down with illnesses that I gave in and admitted how I felt. It was just such a relief to let go of all my emotions and admit I felt hurt and betrayed."
Sue (23)

"I never had a job when my husband was alive but once he'd gone, I'd find myself wasting whole afternoons pondering on our past. Once, when I managed to waste a complete week just reliving memories, I knew I had to do something or I'd waste away. So I got a small voluntary job to occupy myself. Doing things and helping other people takes my mind off myself and what's happened. It's wonderful to start living again."
Elizabeth (50)

The way you wear your hat,

The way you sip your tea,

slurp
gulp
slurp

The memory of all that,
Oh No, they can't take
that away from me.
. . . . Unfortunately.

(2) Talking about your memories and how you can't get them out of your mind is, surprisingly, the best way to rid yourself of them. You may think this will be a burden to your friends, but ask yourself, 'What friend wouldn't listen in a time of need?' Talk to your friends.

"Being single, anytime a friend is breaking up I get the phone call or the visit. I listen and listen. When it gets really repetitive I become less sympathetic. However, everyone needs time just to pour it out. Friends gave me that time, now I give it back."
Mary (40)

Of course, it can be difficult to stand back and see memories for what they really are – our mind's way of slowly working through the pain and distress of our loss. Memories are an expression of our inner struggle to let go of the past. One part of us screams, "Forget it. Let me block it all out," while the other clings on for dear life. The result is an unrelenting mix of thinking you're over "him" but knowing in your heart of hearts you're not. The truth is you can carry on living without foregoing your memories. It's far healthier to let yourself grieve about what's happened than try to block it all out.
(3) While some reminiscing can have a positive value (i.e., in helping you find out where things have gone wrong), going over and over the break-up and wishing things had been different will not help you. Moan to your friends about it, and then stop brooding and get on with the future.

"After spending a month complaining and crying to my friends, I decided it was time to stop nursing my broken heart and get on with my life. I think I came to a crossroads where I thought I either go on like this forever or I move forward."
Karen (32)

2. How to Cope When Loneliness Hits You

Almost everyone will admit to feeling lonely at some point in their life. It is because of this that many of us choose to remain in unfulfilling relationships rather than taking the risk of being alone. Studies on loneliness show it is a direct result of lack of human contact and communication. A state we can all fall into for a number of reasons, but something that hits harder when you suddenly find yourself single once more.

The bitterest loneliness of all comes from the loss of a shared life. A disaster or a triumph can no longer be shared, everything seems somewhat darker. There are times when you're going to feel sad, and lonely. In small doses, this is natural, and having a good cry is healthy. No-one expects you to be a ray of sunshine the whole time. As long as your friends can see you're trying they're not going to mind you lapsing into down moments now and again. Being alone means you take control of your life, do what you want, accept signs of friendship and live by the rule that everything you give out in life you get back.

A survey by the University of Southern California in the early 1980s showed that loneliness was ranked fifth overall as a health hazard by the 1000 students in the survey. 71% claimed it was a danger to health and 250 admitted to feeling lonely at least once a day. High statistics, but then again hardly very surprising. In this rat race age, people love to keep themselves busy, busy, busy. We're all guilty of it. We like to fill our diaries with appointments both social and otherwise in the hope that we won't have to spend time by ourselves. It's almost as if most of us are trying to outrun loneliness, thinking if we keep still for one moment it'll get us. Thus, it is also the uncommunicative busy aspect of our lives that causes loneliness, not just being on our own.

"When my boyfriend left me, I felt so lonely all the time. I couldn't bear to be alone; I would fill up all my hours, seeing friends, going to parties and restaurants. But my feelings of loneliness just got worse and worse. I'd find myself in the middle of a mass of chattering people with nothing to say. So I'd just stand there feeling useless and lonely."
Jennifer (35)

Part of the trouble is, most of us need constant reassurance to help us revive our flagging confidence. We need people to tell us that we're nice, that we're special and more importantly that we're loved. When you're part of a couple this comes naturally and very obviously in the form of physical contact. However, when you become single, whether it was your choice or not, this security is suddenly taken away. Your ego is crushed, you feel unloved,

abandoned and what's worse still, you have long hours alone to ponder on it. But loneliness doesn't just rear its ugly head when we're alone. It can attack anywhere. Who hasn't been in a crowd of people or in a relationship and suddenly felt very lonely.

"There were times when I would be standing in the kitchen with my kids and my husband and I'd just feel very lonely. It was a horrible nagging emptiness that I couldn't get rid of. It would stay in the pit of my stomach and gnaw away at my self-confidence. I know what it was saying. It said, what are you doing with your life?"
Susan (45)

Learning to rebuild your self-confidence will help you to cope with your loneliness by making you realise you can do something positive about it.
(1) Realise that nothing has changed about you. Just because you're single again, doesn't mean that you've become a person with no personality.
(2) Admit to your friends that you're lonely. It's very easy to make everyone believe you are happy and busy, when in fact all you do is sit at home alone. Don't let false pride stand in the way of your friends' help.
(3) Make sure you separate the term lonely from being alone. After all, solitude is not loneliness. And being on your own doesn't have to be a negative state. Remember, just because you are no longer part of a couple doesn't mean the world has stopped turning, there are still hundreds of things to do and lots of people to see.

"I was terrified when I went off to my first pottery lesson. I kept thinking everyone will know each other and be brilliant at pottery. I'll be left alone at the back. But it wasn't like that. The teacher was really nice and so were the people. The things that really made me go for it, were the thought of how lonely I

was at home, and my kids who were all for me going out and doing something positive."
Mary (40)

In the 1990s, the popular view of a single woman is no longer someone who is lonely, miserable, and desperate for a man. Thanks to films like *Thelma and Louise*, *This Is My Life*, *When Harry Met Sally*, *Baghdad Cafe* and books like *Possession* by A.S. Byatt, the *V.I. Warshawki* stories by Sara Paretsky, *Brazzaville Beach* by William Boyd and *Hotel Du Lac* by Anita Brookner.

3. Don't Be Your Own Worst Enemy

Everyone loves a bit of self-pity. Go on, admit it. There's nothing better than surrounding yourself with masses of tissues, watching a truck load of soppy videos and bawling your eyes out. Although this can help you at first, after a while even you'll get fed up so learn to do things positively.
(1) Start thinking for yourself. If you've been in a relationship for a long time, the chances are you're used to someone else sharing the decision making with you. But being by yourself, means having to cope with the day-to-day pressures of life whether you like it or not. This means bills, taxes, jobs, the responsibilities that are halved within a relationship. Learn to ask for help if you can't cope or at least consult an expert. If you had an illness you'd go to the doctor wouldn't you? So when you have a material problem go to the source.

"I was determined at first to prove to everyone how well I was coping. I didn't want anyone to accuse me of being useless on my own. So I pretended everything was fine. But it wasn't and eventually it all came tumbling down around my head."
Sarah (26)

(2) Recognise that you haven't failed. In fact, there is no such thing as failure, just varying degrees of success. If something doesn't work out then it doesn't work out and you should forget it and carry on.
(3) Don't run away from your problems. Tempting as it may be to stick your head in the sand, problems never disappear on their own. All it takes is initiative and a bit of courage to face them.

"I thought if I moved away from London, things would be better. I fooled myself into thinking how nice it was not to know anyone, not to be afraid that someone down the road knew I had failed with my marriage. Finally after three years alone, I realised that I was more scared to live now, than I had been when my relationship first broke up."
Jenny (32)

(4) Whatever you do, don't brood on why he left you or why things went wrong. Realise that in order to be a "good" person you don't have to be perfect. We all have faults, we all do things we're ashamed of, we do all these things because we're human and it's normal. The world is often unfair and our best points are always left unnoticed. Isn't it strange how people always choose to remember bad things about each other rather than good things? Make yourself one of the people who remember good things, and people will offer you the same chance.

4. Going On When You Don't Want to

At first becoming single again is a depressing and overwhelming time, and one which is very hard to pull out of. The main sign of this stage is apathy, not wanting to do anything or see anyone.

"I remember going through a stage when I gave up. I didn't want to do anything. I wouldn't eat, I wouldn't go out, I'd just sit indoors all day refusing to let myself feel anything. I just didn't want to go on, life was too painful and I didn't want to be a part of it."
Pam (29)

Those who feel like this will probably do everything without enjoyment. They are numb to the world and people who try to pull them out of their apathy.

"I'd hate it when friends and family would come round; they'd say things like, 'snap out of it', 'don't be so pathetic'. All it resulted in doing was making me feel like I was right to be this way."
Julie (38)

It's easy to ask the question, "What's the point" when you feel depressed about life but it's harder to listen to the answer. Of course, there's a point to life! There's even a point to being single again. Remember, if we didn't get burned now and then we'd lack compassion, and understanding. Though it's wretched to feel like this you won't feel like this forever.

"It was only when my daughter said to me, 'You know Mum, Dad died, not you' that I realised how dreadful I was being to my family and myself."
Julie (38)

"It sounds crazy but literally one day I woke up and suddenly things didn't seem so bad. My life was still the same mess but I knew it was up to me to make the most of it and sort it out."
Carla (27)

Time is a great healer. For most single people the loss of a relationship for whatever reason does become less acute as time goes on. The reminders that things have changed lessen, and a new pattern of life evolves. One that is based around yourself and no-one else. Selfish, maybe? Enjoyable – definitely.

"I used to be plagued with memories and loneliness but as I started to set up a new life for myself I thought about my past less and less. Now I'm more surprised when I remember things, than when I don't."
Sian (37)

It is important to remember that you should take your own time. There is no timetable for the heart; pain and upset take a different route through all of us. But acceptance of being single again is a healthy and positive step forward. It doesn't mean you have to stop living, breathing or loving, all it means is your life has changed. Acceptance is also the realisation that we have to risk things and take chances. The person who does not risk anything may avoid the pain of life but she will be a slave to the safe world she has created.

Chapter Three

ANGER AND DEPRESSION

ANGER

1. Why Do You Feel This Way?

So you're angry – in fact you're more than angry, you're furious. You're single and you hate it, even if you chose it, you don't like it. We all know how hard it is not to react with anger when we're frustrated. Think about life when you were a child. If you were denied something you wanted, how did you respond? With the first emotion easily at hand – anger! It's a natural response to being upset, but it's also something that can totally destroy your peace of mind.

In the course of life we all have to learn to deal with our more negative emotions. We're told to control our temper, not show our jealousy and to behave at all times. The trouble is, we don't always feel like behaving, especially when we're hurt and miserable. Who hasn't felt like screaming at the top of their voice in a moment of pure frustrated agony?

"Sometimes, I feel so mad about being single again that I just want to smash everything in my flat."
Francesca (27)

"I've found that I've had to control my anger because it was starting to alienate my friends."
Sharon (30)

Lots of women feel mad as hell when their relationships end and they become single. This anger is often made worse by the fact that it still isn't socially acceptable for women to lose their tempers. However, we have to learn to deal with this feeling because anger is a powerful emotion that can have damaging physiological side effects whether you suppress it or let it explode.

"I have a real problem with my anger. I was brought up to believe that it's unladylike to scream and yell, so I bottled up all my fury about being ditched and let it seethe away inside me. The end result is I feel hard done by all the time."
Karen (34)

"After my divorce I would get angry all the time. My blood pressure would build up over the smallest thing and I'd look like a bright red tomato that was about to explode. Apart from being unattractive, it would give me a very uncomfortable feeling in my chest. My doctor said, if I didn't deal with it, I would damage my health."
Sue (40)

2. Temper and More Temper

"It's so easy for me to get angry about my divorce. I just have to sit there and think of all the terrible things I've had to put up with, the lack of money I've now got and the way my kids are suffering. But at the end of the day it doesn't do any good. It doesn't make me feel any better, and it doesn't change a single fact. In fact, it just makes the whole world look worse."
Anne (38)

We're all very good at thinking about the negative aspects of our world, it makes us feel that we're being "realistic" when in fact all we're doing is being pessimistic. If you're angry about being single and choose to see your new world full of worry, misery and loneliness, it will be. This will

QUITE FRANKLY I DON'T GIVE A DAMN EITHER!

make you even angrier and as a result you'll feel even more frustrated and unhappy. The other side of the coin is to use your anger to your advantage, admit you feel bad and vent it in a positive way.

A final point to watch out for is that people respond to you in the way you respond to them. If you rush about being angry in the face of help and blaming everyone for your problems, people will return your venom. If you learn to control your temper, you'll be amazed at how calm and at ease the people around you will be.

3. Revenge

Revenge springs not from what has occurred but from our feelings of hurt and pride, it is a resounding reaction to the thought – "I don't deserve to be treated this way!"

We've all read such stories of anger and revenge in the paper. They run from the laughable – "Woman runs up £10,000 phone bill at her ex-boyfriend's flat" to the downright scary – "Wife kills ex-husband and his new wife".

"When my husband left me for another woman I was mad. I hated him for treating me so despicably and I hated myself for letting him. Because I had kicked him out, his clothes were still at my house. In a fit of anger one morning I cut all his suits up. When I realised what I had done, I was even more frustrated because I knew I'd bought him the suits in the first place."
Maria (30)

Being malicious and filling your brain with thoughts of revenge won't bring your relationship back, it will only increase your unhappiness. If a fire was burning outside your house you wouldn't pour petrol on it. Likewise, if you're angry about being left, making yourself seethe about it will make it worse.

4. Why Anger is Good for You

Although many people say anger should be avoided they are wrong. It should always be controlled, but it should never ever be avoided and suppressed. In any case, unless you're one of the Stepford Wives, you're unlikely to be able to go through life without ever feeling anger pass through your veins.

Anger can actually be a safety valve, a sort of self-defence to stop people taking advantage of you. You usually feel it when someone is picking on you or when someone isn't holding up their side of a bargain. Everyone

feels angry in different ways. Being angry about becoming single is a direct result of the way you got into this situation in the first place.
(1) If your boyfriend/husband left you for someone else, you're likely to be angry for being left behind or for being made to feel inferior even when you know you're not.
(2) If you've suffered a bereavement, then your anger may stem from your feelings of abandonment, no matter how unjust you know it is.
(3) Even if you chose to become single, you may feel angry that you had to make that choice.

Whatever your reasons, your anger is there and has to be dealt with.

If you repress it, it will only emerge at a later time in your life. Pretending you don't feel unhappy and/or mad is a sure fire way to court disaster; instead, confront your pain head on.
(1) Let your anger build up to a certain level, then do something about it, like dig the garden, exercise like mad or go swimming.
(2) Think: what better revenge is there, than to make a success of your life without "him". To really show him that you can succeed without any help.
(3) Let all the anger energise you. Do some voluntary work, enrol in some classes. Write all those letters you've been meaning to write for ages. You could even write a letter to him, which you don't have to post. Burn it or read it again after three days. It might even make you laugh.

"My boyfriend was always fond of telling me how useless and pathetic I was at everything. When he left me, I was so angry that I became determined to show him that not only could I cope on my own but I could succeed brilliantly as well."
Anna (30)

"When I first became single I was angry about everything. I'd snap at anyone who came near me and be angry and behave badly anywhere I was. It was only when I started going to see a counsellor that I realised it was easier to behave like this than cope with my fear of being alone."
June(29)

Turning the energy from your anger into assertion will make you feel a hundred times better. You'll certainly find you'll sleep better. If you feel you've been treated badly then say so. Of course, writing a letter or making a telephone call won't bring "him" back to you but it will get your anger out of your system and allow you to get on with your new life.

(4) Dealing with what upsets you is the only way to get rid of it. If that means going for counselling therapy, or moving, or facing someone, then do it. It's your life and you have to live it as you know best.

"For years I wouldn't admit that I was furious about Bob running off with my friend. I made a real effort to get on with my life, got married to a lovely man and was happy. But something inside of me would just make me feel so depressed at times and I couldn't put my finger on it. Then one day I bumped into Bob at a local shop. He asked how I was and for some reason I just lost it and yelled and yelled at him. I thought for a while it was because I still loved him, but then I realised I was only getting my anger about being ditched so nastily out of my system. I feel great now."
Adele (33)

The now famous writer/screenwriter, Nora Ephron, got over her cheating husband and subsequent divorce by writing a book about her life with him. Entitled *Heartburn*, it also became a successful film.

5. How to Vent Your Fury

Dare I say it, but this can actually be a fairly enjoyable experience; many people compare it to exorcising their souls. As has already been discussed, releasing your anger in a positive way is good for you. It releases all your pent-up emotions and clears a space within you to carry on. Put a time aside to vent your anger and tears and you'll soon be on the road to recovery.
(1) The first step is finding a place to do it. If you have thin walls in your house or share a flat, at least make sure your neighbours and/or flatmates are out.
(2) Next, make sure you vent your fury on inanimate things. Pillows are good for punching, as are beds.

Tearing up old sheets, smashing useless plates and tearing up photos are also very popular.
(3) Screaming is wonderful for getting rid of pent-up fury! Again make sure you do it far away from anyone, or at least warn someone. One woman I know took up the saxophone and every time she got a letter from her husband's lawyer, she'd grab the instrument and blow really hard, till she had no energy left to be angry.
(4) Ask your friends for tips on how they vent their fury. Below is a list of some of the things women interviewed for this book felt really help.

"I took up gardening and every time I was really mad, I'd stalk around my garden cutting the heads off flowers, yanking out weeds and viciously mowing the lawn. I probably have the worst garden in the neighbourhood, but I bet I'm the sanest person around."
Naomi (30)

"I'd get in the car and drive. Anywhere, it didn't matter. With the windows closed and the radio up, I could scream and scream and no-one could hear me. It gets rid of all my stress."
Jenni (28)

"I always get down on my hands and knees and clean my house, even if it doesn't need it. I wash windows, scrub floors, and sing very very loudly."
Annie (40)

"I just go out and shop like crazy. Not a very good thing when you haven't got money. But there's nothing like spoiling yourself like crazy when you're mad."
Sue (29)

"I do all the things I know are bad for me, like smoke, drink and eat great big cream cakes. Then I sit and laugh because I feel so much better."
Mary (40)

DEPRESSION

1. Suppressed Anger

Depression is often suppressed anger. It is the worst kind of anger because often we don't recognize it as anger. The most important thing you can do is examine why you feel so depressed. Write down what you feel depressed about, and pick one thing to get angry about. See if you can make yourself feel really cross. Try and build it up and then re-read the section on venting your fury!

2. Boredom

What's the plague of childhood that follows us around when we're down? Boredom, that's what! When you're part of a couple it's easy to sit around and be happy doing nothing. You can lie on the sofa and feel entertained. Unfortunately, when you are alone you know you have to make your own entertainment because boredom becomes more of an issue.

Before, you were practically guaranteed a partner if you wanted to go to the cinema or a restaurant; now you may feel you have to find a partner every time you want to go out. Unfortunately, depression goes hand in hand with boredom. This is why people who are unemployed become so down. There is a great temptation to do nothing all day so life can seem dismal.

We all know how hard it is to go out and about when you've got no-one to go with. People seem to look at you

with a certain amount of pity, especially when you sit in a restaurant alone. The hardest thing to cope with is the fact that you may not enjoy yourself even if you do go out. If this happens don't give up. Everything is frightening the first time you do it, but that's what makes it exciting.

"The first time I went to the cinema alone I felt awful. I was conscious that I was alone with my popcorn while everyone else was in twos and threes. I felt everyone's eyes were on me and when the lights when down I bolted for the door as if I had done something awful. But I went back and now I realise that lots of people, single or otherwise, do things alone."
Julie (29)

3. Lifting Yourself Out of a Depression

Don't let yourself fall into a depression about being alone, take some positive action. Try and do things. Simply getting out of the house or flat can help.

(1) If you want to go to a restaurant but are afraid of being stared at, the solution to this is to take a book or a magazine with you. Not only does it give you something to do but it also stops you avoiding the gaze of all those people at other tables. And remember, if you don't feel lonely and awkward, no-one will look at you that way.
(2) The cinema is always a good choice, you can't talk in there anyway so you don't need a partner. The theatre is the same, as is the ballet.
(3) If you aren't artistically inclined, then how about something more exercise-based. Many a true friendship has been made at the gym or at an aerobics class. If anything it's an excellent way to make new friends.
(4) Or how about an all girls night for both single girls and those in a relationship.

(5) A dinner party can also be fun, as can a picnic on a sunny day.
(6) Day trips to other towns or shopping adventures are also great for relieving depression.

Change is uncomfortable and getting used to being alone is very like getting into a new relationship; remember, if at first you don't succeed, try, try, try again.

Chapter Four

FRIENDS

1. Friends are a Goldmine

"No man is a failure who has friends"; so says James Stewart in the film *It's A Wonderful Life*. Never a truer point was made. Think what your life would be like without friends. It would be worse than being without a boyfriend because you'd have no-one to go to when things got tough, and no-one to tell you when you're being a moany old boot. If you're still not convinced, imagine what it would be like if your best friend moved away. Suddenly, there'd be no-one to eat cold pizza with, no-one to read *Hello* with and worse still, no-one to share those inane comments or have a giggle with.

If you're even going to attempt to survive the single life, you've got to learn to depend on one thing – friends! They are a goldmine and if you treat them right will stick by you for life. It's important first of all to create a circle of friends for yourself. Once you have different types of friends for the different parts of your life, you'll never be lonely and short of company. Of course, some people get by on having one good friend and while this is brilliant, the downside is what would you do if he/she decided to move away? You'd be back at square one, single and with no friends. It's far better to cultivate a network of people you can turn to whatever your mood.

Sometimes, people don't realise that they already run their lives this way. If you're not sure how your friends measure up, try this quick three-point guide:

(1) The first step in enlarging your circle of friends or determining who they are is to write down a list of the things you like doing. Be honest, it's no point trying to convince yourself that you like pot-holing when you wouldn't be seen dead crawling into anything besides your bed. The chances are you'll have at least five things on your list, eg: film, sports, cooking, theatre, shopping.
(2) Then write a list of all the people you know (they don't have to be bosom buddies) and try and match up people to the subjects you like doing. If you look closely you'll probably have at least one friend for each thing you enjoy. This means whenever you feel like doing one thing from your first list, you'll have at least one person you can ask to accompany you.
(3) If this doesn't work then it's time to join some clubs. This may seem like a frightening thought but it really isn't so bad. If you enjoy watching films then the best place to meet someone with similar interests is a film club, or a film course. Don't worry about not knowing what to say, remember you're meant to be doing something you supposedly enjoy, so of course, you'll have something to talk about.

"I always wanted to learn to paint when I was younger but there was never any time when my husband was alive. I wanted to take it up after he died but none of my friends were interested, so I took the plunge and did it. I've now met some really interesting people and made friends with one lovely lady called Pat. In fact we're both going to Rome together this summer to see the Sistine Chapel."
Mary (45)

It's important to realise that it's fine to have different sorts of friends and friendships. Not everyone has to be your best friend for life. There are fair-weather friends, friends you admire, friends you go out with, old friends and

...You'll look back on this as your post-husband constructive period...

friends you can rely on to move mountains if need be. They are all important and should all be cherished. When you first become single you may find that the friends you made when you were a couple, are not really your friends any more. This is very common and though upsetting at the time, you should view it as a good sign. After all, at least now you know who your real friends are.

"I had so many friends when I was going out with Karl. Once we split up they all disappeared into the woodwork. I once heard one of them say at a party, 'Liz isn't so interesting now she's not going out with Karl'. I was so hurt but at least I found out who I could trust and who I couldn't."
Liz (26)

It's terrible when friends seem to turn against you but it is possible to safeguard yourself. Like any relationship, you have to work at friendships so they can grow. This means keeping in touch and communicating. Being passive in a relationship and letting your friend do all the running is like sending a message to her that says, "I can't be bothered and I'm not interested". Put yourself in her/his place – not very encouraging, is it? If you look after your friends, whether you're married/single/divorced/living together etc., and don't discreetly forget about them when you become part of a couple, then they'll always stick by you. Just ask any of your single friends about their friends and you'll hear them say everything from "I couldn't live without them", to "They saved my life".

2. Asking for Help

Pride is a funny human trait we all possess. You know what they say, "Pride comes before a fall". It is this reaction which stops us from admitting when we're wrong, and when we're hurt, and more importantly when we need

help. There's something about it that makes us think holding our head high while all the world crumbles around us is the best way to survive. Of course it isn't!

"I broke up with my boyfriend two weeks before I told anyone. I suppose I felt kind of ashamed and didn't want anyone to know. Even when I told my friends I just sort of dropped it into the conversation casually. After that day, I would still pretend I was okay and coping brilliantly with the break-up. It was only when I heard that my best friend had bumped into my daughter and she innocently said 'Mummy cries every night' that I realised I'd been stupid not to ask for help sooner."
Louise (32)

"After I broke up with my boyfriend I cried and cried for the whole night. The next morning my eyes were so swollen that I had to wear sunglasses to work. Everyone kept asking me what was wrong with my eyes, so I lied and said it was an allergic reaction to garlic. I was too embarrassed to tell them I had been ditched. I didn't want anyone to feel sorry for me. It's only later when I told them, that I realised if I'd told them right at the beginning I wouldn't have spent so many days by myself crying my eyes out."
Jenni (26)

The whole point of having friends is that they are there for the good times and the bad. If they are real friends, they won't care too much in an absolute emergency if you need them at 3 am or at 3 pm, all you have to do is ask for help. There's nothing better when you feel mad about being single to get them round, and moan on to them. Learn to lean on your friends. It doesn't mean that you should lean so much that you're living in their house 24 hours a day, 365 days a year, rather that you learn to turn to them when things are particularly bad. No-one is going to think you're weak (least of all your friends) if you ask a friend to come round and stay for a while. Likewise, they aren't going to get mad at you when you need advice or someone to listen to you. It actually takes a far stronger person to admit they need help, than someone who pretends everything is all right.

"All my friends thought he was wrong for me in the first place so I felt when he left that I couldn't then turn to them, without one of them saying, 'I told you so'. But they were great, they really stuck by me and just helped me get through it. I can't believe how lucky I am to have friends like these."
Georgia (38)

Ask yourself, do you think you're a good friend? The chances are your answer will be yes. Well, part of being a good friend is letting your friends help when you're feeling bad. There's nothing worse than being pushed away by a friend when all you want to do is help. Your friends can see you're in pain so let them do their bit. Anyway it can be fairly enjoyable to be clucked over and have someone to mop up your tears. It can also be quite refreshing to hear someone else say, "He wasn't right for you" besides yourself. Talking to someone and voicing your thoughts can be reassuring because it lets you know that there is someone on your side. It is also constructive to hear what someone else who knows you, thinks of what has happened.

Learning to rely on your friends when you're single is part of making yourself strong again. Actually going through difficult times together also brings friends closer and strengthens relationships. No-one expects you to lead a solitary life whereby no-one is allowed to enter your own private sphere. Who can live like that? Who wants to live like that?

3. Accepting Advice

Possibly, you're now at that stage whereby lamenting about your state of affairs has become second nature. If you're not sure if you're at this point take a look at your friends. Do their eyes glaze over when you bring up the subject of being single again? Do they sigh exasperatedly when you refuse once again to come out? Have they run out of kleenex, toilet roll and any soakable substance for you? If you answered yes to any of these questions, it is probably time that you sat up and listened to their advice.

Everyone is allowed to have their mourning period to get over loss and while this varies from person to person, if your friends see that you are not doing anything to help yourself, their patience will wear thin. Bear this in mind when friends don't always say what you want them to say.

Sometimes, the things they say may even hurt, but as long as you know them well enough and know they have your best interests at heart then you should listen to their advice. After all, it's very easy to use self-pity as an escape route when you become single, we all know that it's easier to sit inside and wallow in misery than get out there and do something positive and worthwhile. This is where friends come in handy. They can administer the kick in the butt we all need at times.

"It was only when a group of my friends came round and basically told me I was turning into a miserable couch potato that I sat up and took notice. I mean these were the girls who had been my crutch only two months ago and now they were basically telling me to get off my lazy arse and do something. Of course, they were right!"
Sharon (32)

If we can't rely on our friends to dish out much needed advice even when we don't need it, who can we rely on?

However, listening to advice doesn't necessarily mean taking all the advice at face value. Put your own gut feeling first and mix it with what your friends are saying.

"Lots of my friends used to say, go and find yourself a new boyfriend. There are plenty more fish in the sea. While this is true, I knew the last thing I needed right now was another boyfriend. But they were right in one way, I had to stop moaning about what had happened and get on with my life."
Maria (30)

Your friends aren't going to ditch you just because you don't always take their advice, but they may well give up on you, if all you choose to do in life is sit in your flat and let your life turn into a pigsty. Remember you've asked for their help, now take it. Imagine how frustrating it would be if you kept on sympathetically giving help to a friend who refused to see reason. In the end you'd give up, wouldn't you? So don't let your friends walk away and don't be your own worst enemy. Listen to the people around you and learn from what they are saying.

"It's funny but everyone has their own way of getting over heartbreak. My friends and I would all sit down and list our favourite ways of getting over things. It's actually quite strange what people come up with. Some of my friends said completely re-decorating their houses, or moving, helped. While others said, doing something outrageous. In amongst all their suggestions I found a few that really helped me."
Anna (38)

4. Utilising Your Friendships

Now that you've learned it's possible to survive a break-up, it's time you used your friendships to the best advantage. Don't just think of friends as people you can sometimes go to the cinema with.

(1) Make them part of your life – an extended family you can go to whether you're happy, sad, or in-between. For many people, friends are the only family they have and making them a fully fledged member of their lives is extremely important.

"My family live in Australia so when I found myself single again, my kids and I were particularly lonely. Thank goodness I had friends over here. It helps to have people you care about around you, not only for social events and holidays but also for those times when you want to share something special."
Annie (35)

"My children found it particularly hard not having a dad around. If it wasn't for some of my friends I don't know what I'd have done. They're great, always coming round to help me fix things, playing with the kids when I have to go to work, even making times like Christmas and birthdays really special with lots of people."
Clare (40)

"I try to see becoming single as the best thing that's happened to me. It's made me realise how lucky I am to have such good friends. I thought my life was over when I split up with my boyfriend, but it wasn't. All that was over was a part of it. I still have my job, I still have my health and more importantly, I still have my friends."
Louise (32)

(2) Listen to their problems too; after all, a one-sided

relationship is never healthy. Give and take is what makes relationships and friendships really work. So ask them how they are and really listen to what they say. Not only will it put your problems into perspective but it will also take your mind off yourself and make you feel useful.

"I feel quite guilty now. I used to go on and on to my best friend about how depressed I was and how I missed my husband. Then one day I found her in tears and discovered that her mother had cancer. It was then I'd realised what a terrible friend I had been, always going on about myself and never thinking for one minute that she had problems of her own."
Donna (33)

(3) Be interested in their lives as well. When you always see a friend on a one-to-one basis it becomes easy to forget about the rest of the world and think that no-one else matters. But in the same way, just as being happily ensconced with a boyfriend/husband without regard for anyone else is bad, so too is this. It's important when you're single again to widen your circle of friends. This means meeting their friends and taking the plunge going out with people you don't know. Look closely at your friends; the chances are you met them through someone else, so who knows who you'll meet through them.

"I never wanted to meet Elaine's friends because they all sounded too highbrow for me. But when I became single again and needed her, I realised we would never be close if I didn't make an effort with her other friends. Now I'm glad I did because I've made so many new friends."
Francesca (27)

(4) Make plans with them. Part of utilising your friendships, is never thinking of yourself as an imposition or a

charity case. Even friends who are in relationships will be willing to do things away from their partners; after all, everyone needs a break now and then. So go ahead and plan a holiday together or decide to do a course together. But be careful and don't allow yourself to become a stop-gap for those friends of yours who are in relationships. If you find a friend only wants you around when her boyfriend is busy or when she hasn't got one, do yourself a favour and find someone who really likes you and values your company. A true friend will want to see you regardless of whether she's single or not.

"Every year now, I go away for a week with my two best friends. We just go somewhere cheap and have a laugh for a week. One of them is married, the other in and out of relationships, but we still keep that one week apart for ourselves. It's nice. It's like saying we're as important to each other as our families are."
Susan (45)

(5) Spoil your friends. Don't be embarrassed to buy small gifts and send cards to the people you love. Choosing a gift or doing a nice deed for someone you like is a lovely feeling. From their point of view, it lets them know they're on your mind, and they're special. From your point of view it will make you feel happy and secure that you've got people around who you feel close to.

"I love spoiling my friends, it makes me feel so happy to be able to give them things. It's like letting them know I put them on a par with my family and treasure their friendship. It's also nice because I do it because I want to, not because I feel I have to like I did when I was married."
Sharon (30)

Chapter Five

BE YOUR OWN BEST FRIEND

1. Being Fit for Life

Learning to look after yourself can be quite a trial. We all know it's easier to become a couch potato and cocoon yourself inside your cosy house or flat than go out and face the world as a single person. Breaking up and becoming single again, actually feels like the perfect excuse to majorly slob out and let yourself go. After all, there's no-one around to notice how good you look or anywhere to go, so why bother?

Why indeed? Even though everyone has a different idea of what health is and how healthy they'd like to be. There are certain things that need to be addressed if you want to be fit for life. And before you deny it, you do want to be fit for life because once you are, you'll look at life through different eyes. So what is being fit for life? Well it isn't feeling tired when you get up, having no energy and getting headaches through the day. It is a real sense of health and a general feeling of mental and physical wellbeing. This doesn't mean you have to become fitter than Jane Fonda or cleverer than Einstein. It means you should aim for a state of health you feel comfortable with.

So if at this moment you're sitting there reading this book, with lank dirty hair, shapeless clothes and an attitude to match someone out of *Eastenders*, then it's time to change your ways.

(1) Making the most of yourself, wherever you are and whatever you're doing, will keep your spirits up. Feeling unattractive even if you are by yourself is a real self-esteem killer.

Chocco BAR!

"When I first got divorced it was easier for me to lounge about on my own looking like a slob than do anything remotely body conscious. It was only when I caught sight of myself in the mirror one day that I realised how I'd let myself go. I'd put on weight, my hair was disgusting and I felt terrible. That made my life even worse, so I decided to do something about myself, and instead of putting all my energies into moaning I put them into making the best of myself. It was the best thing I ever did."
Pat (40)

(2) Learn that what is ideal for one person isn't necessarily ideal for you. So what if your friend works out five times a week, eats only carrots and has a body like an ironing board? Ask yourself, would you feel happy this way? Probably not. Being fit doesn't mean you have to starve yourself and force yourself to do things you hate.

"I've learnt that becoming a fit person means doing things in moderation. I used to work out all the time and became obsessed with my body. It was almost as if I had exchanged obsessing about my ex-boyfriend to obsessing about my looks. So I cut down on my workouts and learned to spend more time doing a variety of different things."
Josie (28)

(3) Exercise your mind. This means use your head. It's a well-known fact that stretching your mind will make you feel active. Not only will it relieve boredom but it will give you something to get your teeth into. Everyone has something they're interested in and if you can't afford to buy books on the subject, check out your local library. Start by reading; if you don't fancy wading through a book, buy a couple of magazines or aim to read at least one paper all the way through every day. Not only will this give your mind something to think about besides being

single, it will also give you something to talk about when you do go out. It's also very surprising how well read you can become in a short time.
(4) Learn to use your local council to its full advantage. Not only do they have details of local courses and colleges but they also put you in touch with colleges in different areas. It is also a good place to meet people and really discover what you're interested in.

"When I got divorced I realised that I hadn't touched a book since I left college. I used to be really interested in history and art and somehow I gave it all up over the years. Becoming single again was the perfect time for me to get back into it. It got rid of all my newly acquired spare time and at the same time it made me feel like I was doing something useful with my life."
Karen (33)

"It was my kids who encouraged me to go back to college. They kept nagging me that sitting in the house on my own and doing nothing all day was bad for me. And they were right; I went from being an active person when my husband was alive to doing nothing after his death. Now I enjoy life more. I've found going out and doing something positive has made me do more things than I've ever done."
Jo (40)

(5) Learn to settle for less than perfect. This means don't set yourself impossible goals that you'll never reach. I'm all for striving for the best but attempting to look like Cindy Crawford when you're 5ft 4in just isn't going to happen. Most of us aren't born with model looks but this doesn't mean we can't be emotionally and physically healthy. If you have a good look at the people you admire, the chances are it isn't their looks which make them attractive. Success, self-confidence and personality are

what makes a person attractive. You could look like a million dollars but have the personality of a brick and no-one would like you. Strive for what makes you happy in life, not what will please others.

"It was only when I became single again that I realised how much I'd done to please my boyfriend. He liked girls with long hair who were quite feminine and I'm quite a tomboy at heart. Still, it didn't stop me from growing my hair and dressing to please him. It makes me sound quite pathetic, doesn't it? But I bet a lot of women do that. It's nice being single now and doing my own thing. It makes me feel a lot healthier and happier."
Fran (28)

(6) Learning to keep away from alcohol and cigarettes can also be excellent for your health. If you've found that you've become dependent on these substances to the extent that they're taking over your life, there are things you can do about it. Organisations which can help are listed at the end of the book.

2. Eating Properly

Food – is it the joy or the nightmare of your life? For some people food can be a great comfort when they're upset, yet for others it's something they never think of. Becoming single means re-educating yourself to eat properly. If you've gone through years of cooking for someone else every night, being single may feel like an excuse to stop eating. But even if you've lost your appetite completely you have to eat something. Making sure you have the right food and nutrition will give you the physical strength to go on.

Don't become a junkaholic. Eating vast amounts of junk, like biscuits, cake, chocolate, burgers or anything

yours or mine?
Cat food

else of that ilk will lower your energy levels, make you feel lethargic and ruin your skin, hair and nails. It may be easier to grab a packet of biscuits than cook a meal but in the long run it will destroy your self-confidence.

"My husband left me after my kids went off to college. So suddenly I went from 20 years of cooking every night to not having to cook at all. At first it was bliss – no more menu planning. I would just grab something on my way home. But not only did that prove expensive, it also mean I ate really badly."
Mandy (47)

Healthy eating can help to prevent not only heart trouble but many other illnesses too. Healthy eating doesn't meat eating less of everything. There are certain foods you should get more of, like fibre. You get fibre from meals that include beans, brown rice, pasta and vegetables. People often think that starchy foods like bread, pasta and rice are fattening but this isn't true. It's the things you use with them that are usually fattening. If you're working on a budget, products like tinned beans, baked potatoes, brown rice and brown bread and fruit are very good for you. Using semi-skimmed milk, cheese with half fat and butter with no salt are also good for you. Try to eat white meat instead of red and use yoghurt instead of cream. None of these products will mean radical changes for you if you eat a balanced diet already and what's more, they don't cost any more and can easily be bought from your local supermarket.

Eating properly protects us from stress, damaging illnesses and tension. It can also be quite an enjoyable process and one which will change the way you look at your life. Don't see eating properly as a temporary measure, see it as part of the process of reconstructing a new, healthier and happier lifestyle for yourself.

"When I became single again, I decided I was going to change my life for the better. That meant not only changing the things around me like my flat and job but also changing myself. I have always been slim but I knew I was a junk eater if there was no-one around to bully me into eating healthily. I thought it was about time I stopped relying on other people to make me do things and started shopping properly. Now I find it's easier to eat healthily than to eat badly. It's done two things for me: one, it's made me realise I could set myself a goal and achieve it; and two, I've never felt so good."
Jill (36)

3. Changing Your Image

The way you present yourself to the outside world is reflective of how you think of yourself. We all tend to let ourselves go when we feel miserable. It's all part of the lethargy of depression. But a change is as good as a rest, or so they say. Lots of women decide that becoming single again is a good excuse to change their images completely, do away with the past and start afresh, and why not? Learning to cherish yourself for yourself is an important part of being single again.

"When I left my boyfriend I decided the first thing I was going to do was cut my hair. It was such a feeling of freedom to have it all chopped off. It made me feel like I was starting afresh – a new woman."
Stephanie (34)

(1) Start by putting apart at least one day a month to spoil yourself. You could start by a trip to the hairdressers. If you can't afford to pay for the full whack why not go along on a models' night. This is the trainee night that most salons have at least once a month. Forget the horror stories, good salons keep a fervent watch on their trainees

and won't let them butcher your hair. A tip here – never go into a hairdressers and say "do what you want" unless you want a totally useless hairstyle that you'll never be able to do again. Also, you aren't likely to end up with something *you* want. So, have some sort of idea when you go in. Check out the hair magazines and ask your friends what they think.

Learn to really spoil yourself occasionally – if your idea of this is lying in the bath with music blaring and stuffing a McDonald's down your mouth, and swigging a bottle of wine, then do it. There's no-one around to moan at you, call you a disgusting pig or make you feel guilty in any way. I don't suggest you make a habit of it, but once a month isn't going to kill you.

(2) Change your wardrobe (no, not literally). Open those doors and really have a good look at all the clothes in there. I'll just bet half the clothes in there have never seen the light of day, or are so old that they'll fall apart if you wash them again. Be stern with yourself and chuck out anything

you don't wear or aren't likely to wear again. A painful process but one which will be very worthwhile. It will make space for all your new clothes and if you take them along to Oxfam or another charity shop, it will have the added bonus of making you feel self-righteous for a while.

Now it's time to look for some new clothes. It doesn't have to be an expensive process. There are plenty of national shops that specialise in warehouse seconds clothes. Shops like Mark One and What She Wants all stock the same clothes as the big chain fashion stores but at much cheaper prices. If this is still out of your range, how about markets or second-hand shops? Many a beautiful bargain has been picked up at a stall or in a jumble sale. No longer is there any stigma to wearing second-hand togs, in fact it's positively trendy these days.

(3) Join a gym. Contrary to popular belief gyms aren't full of Arnold Schwarzeneggar types pumping iron. These days you're more likely to find Mr. Bean types and your average everyday person doing their stuff.

"I was really surprised when I joined the gym, because I've always felt quite shy about my body. It's fairly lumpy and I thought all the people there would have perfect physiques compared to mine. But I joined a beginners aerobics class and to my delight found everyone there was just like me."
Helen (38)

And it doesn't have to be an expensive endeavour; after all, most leisure centres do very cheap rates and if you have young children there is nearly always a crèche service available.

If you don't fancy joining a gym, then the best way to keep really fit is to exercise the whole body. Exercise in the form of running, swimming, walking or cycling is actually much better for you than weightlifting because physical fitness doesn't mean muscular power. So why should you exercise? Well, for a start it will help you to meet new people, get your body into shape and give you more energy.

"I love going to the gym, it gives me energy and makes me feel like I've achieved something every day before I go out. I've never felt better or fitter in my life. It's actually given me a much needed confidence boost that I never had before."
Jenni (28)

4. Expanding Your Horizons

"I always wanted to go to college and get some exams. I got married so young that I never had a chance to study. By the time I was 21 I had three kids and no time on my hands. It's only now at 45 that I've gone back to college and realised what I could have achieved all those years ago. Of course I was nervous about going back but you'd be surprised at how many mature students there are at college these days."
Hannah (45)

"My boyfriend always said I had a terrible voice whenever I tried to sing. He'd say I sounded like a cat being strangled, and though I laughed it hurt quite a bit. I mean I've loved singing since I was a kid. It was only when he left me that I decided to take singing lessons. At my first lesson, my teacher said I had a nice voice; that really lifted my spirits. It's nice to be told you're good at something you love."
Janie (32)

"I've spent 20 years of my life cooking meals for my family and hated every minute of it. But it was the only thing I was good at, so I decided I was going to set up my own catering business. It's still very small and localised but I'm surprised at how much I'm enjoying doing it. It's funny, you hate something for years because you're not doing it for yourself and then you start doing it for you, and it becomes enjoyable."
Jane (42)

"My husband was very good at telling me how I'd never cope without him. And I guess I sort of believed it; after all, I didn't know how to do anything. If he could only see me now with my law degree and know how much I've done. The best thing that ever happened to me was my divorce."
Lucy (30)

Of all the qualities needed to develop self-confidence, risk taking is right up there. If you don't take a risk in life you'll never achieve anything or do anything. This is why you should broaden your horizons and go for your ultimate goal. Taking risks actually involves less trauma in the long run. If you attempt something and fail – so what? At least you've tried and that in itself is a feat. If you never try anything all your life you'll think, "if only . . .".

"I've spent so much time regretting things in my life instead of getting on and doing things. I mean what's the point in

regretting all those years I lived together with Tim, it doesn't matter any more. I've got my own life and my own interests and if I'm really honest I'm happier now than I've ever been. Life's too short for regrets."
Anna (30)

If you want to broaden your horizons and don't know how to make a start, here are a few pointers.
(1) Start by making a list of what you'd like to do with your life. Don't bother to deal with necessities like money and location, you can deal with that later. Just write down anything in your head. Forget about your age or experience. Just believe that anything can be achieved if you set your mind to it. For instance, at 52 years old, Olympia Dukakis decided she was going to be an actress; now she has starred in various successful films like *Steel Magnolias* and even has an Oscar. Writers like Mary Wesley wanted to write for years before they attempted it. She had her first published novel when she was 70 years old.

(2) Find out how you can achieve your goal. Check out your local library, yellow pages and anyone who does what you want to do. It's surprising what you can come up with if you contact your network of friends.
(3) If you want to do something that involves expense, check out how you can do it cheaply. Most local councils have a grant system or a loan system for mature students. Most courses can be done cheaply at a local college and if you try hard enough someone can always be found to give you help. Lots of big companies have information departments and can give you free advice if you need any.
(4) The important thing to remember is that anything can be done as long as you put your mind to it and believe you can do it.

"Half the struggle for me was believing I could do something on my own. For months after I became single again I couldn't even change a light bulb without asking for help. Now I am a real dab hand at DIY."
Jo (28)

(5) Brainstorm with your friends. This means sit down and write down anything you're interested in or would like to learn. It's easier if you do this with friends because they can offer helpful tips and information. Sometimes the most obvious thing will be staring at you straight in the face but you'll need someone else to point it out for you.

5. Think for Yourself

Thinking for yourself means a number of things; for starters it means learning to please yourself. It's hard to bring yourself round to this type of thinking especially if you don't trust yourself. Feeling that your point of view is inferior is a hard habit to break, but one that has to be thwarted if you want to be happily single.

When you are on your own, you are confronted with a number of decisions which you may feel are outside your area and this can be really frightening. But decisions are going to be all around you for the rest of your life so it's important to learn how to cope with them and make decisions for yourself.

Learning to view yourself from a different perspective is also important, because it means instead of thinking of yourself as such and such's girlfriend or someone's wife or lover, you start seeing yourself as a complete person who is more than capable of standing on their own two feet.

"All my life I have been someone's younger sister, or someone's daughter, and then someone's wife. Now for the first time I'm just me and even though that's quite scary it's also quite nice. It fills me with a certain confidence and makes me feel that for the first time my opinion is important."
June (38)

Being different from others and deciding to do something that is completely different is still seen by some as being weird but in a world that seems to demand that people toe the line, it takes courage to be yourself and do things that you want. If you live your life the way others want you to, you'll never feel fulfilled and happy. This is why you have to think for yourself. People are full of useful advice when you're single again, and it's hard to decipher what's right for you and what isn't. The rule to live by is, always do what you want. Listen to that inner voice and if it says no, then listen to it and if it says yes, then go for it.

Of course, there'll have to be times when you compromise but these will be few and far between. Establish your views and what you want and you'll be happy.

"I always admire people who could make decisions at the snap of their fingers. I've never been one of those people. When I

was married I let my husband do all that for me and after the divorce I let my family do it because it seemed easier. It wasn't until I realised that I was forever compromising that I put my foot down and really took control of my life. That means making decisions even though I know they may be unpopular with the people around me. Now if I want quiet because I have to work at home I'll make sure the kids are quiet. If I don't want to see my parents at the weekends because I am busy then I won't. It's hard at first, but once you start doing what's best for you, life becomes easier."
Sharon (32)

6. Overcoming Shyness

Everyone, but everyone, is shy. Even the most boisterous person you know will have times when she is completely dumbfounded and embarrassed and trembling inside. Shyness is a horrible thing, isn't it? It brings waves of panic over even the bravest of people and can stop you from doing nearly anything.

"Becoming single has made my shyness worse. Having my boyfriend leave me has made me feel even more unattractive and uninteresting, so much so that I can't believe anyone would want to talk to me. And when they do it's even worse because I can't think of a single intelligent thing to say."
Alex (35)

Yet, like anything, shyness can be overcome.
(1) The first thing you have to do is stop putting yourself down. Women are particularly good at this; we can take the insults but not the compliments. Learn to believe the nice things people say, and don't insult them by not believing them.
(2) Concentrate on your good points (yes, you do have some!). This means writing a list of all your best points.

Start with modesty if you can't think of anything. Ask your friends for help and believe what they say.
(3) Next, write a list of all the times when you're most shy. Next to each point, try and think what makes you shy. Is it fear? Or lack of confidence? Sometimes, seeing what you feel in black and white makes it easier to deal with.
(4) Don't let your shyness become an excuse to stay at home and do nothing, it will only serve to make things worse.
(5) List all your triumphs and pin them somewhere you can see them. It's easy when we're miserable to forget the successes we've had and only concentrate on the bad.
(6) Set yourself deadlines for tasks and goals. Attempt to overcome at least one aspect of your shyness a month. Start with small things like asking for things in shops to organising a party.
(7) Don't be afraid of failing. The fear of failure is actually worse than failure because it stops you from even trying. If you try at least you'll get somewhere, whereas if you never try you'll get nothing.
(8) If you think the way you look is holding you back from going out there, do something about it. Get fit, get healthy, have your hair cut, etc. Just don't use it as an excuse to not approach people.
(9) Don't apologise all the time. It's a bad habit and people find it very irritating. Standing up for yourself is the first way to get people to respect you and don't let guilt hold you back. Just because you're single doesn't mean you don't deserve to be happy. Punishing yourself for the past won't achieve anything.
(10) Don't be embarrassed when things go wrong. Laugh it off. Not only will this stop other people being embarrassed but it will also let them see what a good sport you are.
(11) When you feel a panic attack coming on, take deep breaths and try to relax and tell yourself that things are

... Are you the Spare Man?

never as bad as they seem. If you are completely dumbfounded and don't know what to say, a tip is to ask questions. There's nothing more flattering than being asked about yourself and it's bound to endear you to your new-found friend.
(12) Don't attempt to achieve this all in one day. Take one day and one task at a time and you'll be fine.

7. Enjoying Your Own Company

One of the hardest parts of being single again is learning to be on your own. Not only do you now have to sleep alone but you also have to eat, think and enjoy being alone.

"I used to wander aimlessly around my house, not knowing what to do or what was missing from my life. Nothing would interest me so I would try to fill each waking hour with as many social appointments as possible, so I wouldn't have to spend any time on my own. As you can imagine, my phone bill was massive."
Maria (34)

Does this sound familiar? Do you find yourself fighting not to be alone? Are you bored the minute you're on your own? Would you rather spend an afternoon with the most boring person you know than be by yourself? If you answered yes to any of these, it's time to start enjoying your own company.

Don't let yourself lead a life full of empty time. If you know you've got time on your hands, prepare for it; this means buying yourself some books for that weekend, deciding what to do with your time once the kids are in bed, or planning ahead and organising things to do for yourself.

"I used to be afraid of being alone, especially on weekends. Then when I split with my boyfriend I realised that it was actually quite nice to be on my own at weekends. It was peaceful and quite a productive time for me. I mean I got to do whatever I wanted, which meant if I wanted to work on a Saturday night then I could and if I wanted to go out then I could do that as well. I didn't have to wait around for anyone else and better still, I didn't have to compromise."
Megan (34)

Ten Things that are Better When You're Single

(1) You can read as late as you want without anyone fussing about the light.
(2) You can chat as long as you like to friends with only the phone bill to worry about, and not someone stomping around in the background.
(3) You can come home from work and not have to listen to anyone's day or be sympathetic when your day was far worse.
(4) The bathroom is all yours (even if you have kids)!
(5) You can listen to *your* CDs and tapes.
(6) You can watch soaps without anyone saying you're missing half a brain.
(7) You can leave the party as early or as late as you like.
(8) You don't have to wash his socks.
(9) You can cook your favourites.
(10) You don't even know the World Cup is on TV!

Chapter 6

COPING WITH EVERYDAY LIFE

1. Handling Your Financial Affairs

Financial affairs can be pretty daunting when you're not used to dealing with them. Are you the sort of person who never knows how much you've got in your bank account and can't find a receipt for anything? If you've answered yes to either of these, it's time to change your ways.

"When my husband died I was completely flummoxed by our financial affairs. He had always paid all the bills, sorted out our joint account and all I had to do was deal with the household account. Suddenly I was left with a mountain of bills, no idea what insurance we had and no idea how to pay for anything. I felt like going to bed and never getting up again."
Joan (45)

"I never realised how I relied on my boyfriend financially till we split up. I couldn't afford to pay the rent on the flat on my own, I couldn't even afford to run my car. The implications of being single and broke were just awful."
Maria (28)

Learning to take responsibility for your financial situation is an important part of taking control of your life. Once you know where you stand money-wise, you'll feel more secure and able to cope with the stresses of everyday life. Learning how to deal competently with finances can only

be an asset in life. And once you master it you'll see that it isn't as complicated and hard as you think it is.

"I've always had a real problem with figures. I was useless at maths at school and when I got married I never had anything to do with our money. Now I'm living alone with a five-year-old to bring up I've had to learn how to deal with problems as they arise. And I'm actually quite surprised at myself – it's not that hard to budget after all."
Lisa (35)

Making yourself take control of your finances is very important if you are determined to make your life work as an independent solo person. Because whether you like it or not, finance is the backbone of all our lives and if you let it fall into disarray, it will totally disrupt everything. If you can't bear to even think about your money situation, look at the problem from a different point of view. Make taking control of your finance a challenge, a skill that you can and will master.

"I was the worst person in the world when it came to money and bills. I thought if I ignored it, it would get better. Instead I found myself getting ill with worry. So I went to my bank and asked for help. My bank manager was so nice; he sat down with me and told me how to keep a record of my expenditure. He also arranged to have my bills paid by standing orders so I wouldn't have a vast sum to pay every quarter. So nowadays even when I don't have much money I don't spend all my time worrying about it. I feel confident about my life because I know I won't have anyone coming round and demanding money off me."
Pam (33)

2. Financial Solvency

(1) Work out a budget for yourself. You don't have to be a mathematical genius to work it out but if it still makes you nervous, try and get someone to help you; everyone knows someone who is okay-ish with their finances. Make sure you're being realistic about what you can afford and what you can't. It's no good promising to pay back £100 a month if you can't afford it. Set yourself easy goals or else you'll be back at square one.

"I felt a lot more comfortable once I had got to grips with what I owed and how much money I had left. Instead of worrying every time I pushed my cashpoint card into the machine, I could work out what I could afford to do and what I couldn't."
Jilly (28)

House
Pension
Insurance
Gas
Chocolate

(2) Go and see your creditors. Banks, credit card companies, landlords and a whole host of other bill collectors, are very willing to help when things go wrong. They actually prefer to know if you're having trouble and when you'll be able to pay them. It's only when you don't contact them that they start to get nasty. They can also help you work out a pay-back scheme as long as you're honest with them. Also, once you've seen them, it will stop all those nasty letters falling through your letter box.

"I was surprised at how much my credit card company would help me. I didn't realise that they had special customer services departments for people who have financial worries."
Pam (35)

(3) Don't be afraid of your bank manager. He may seem like a scary animal about to attack you the moment you walk through the door. But they're normal people like you and me. Just make sure you have worked out what your problems are and know what you're going to do about them.

"When I became single again, one of my biggest worries was paying my bills. I loved my flat and didn't want to lose it but I knew I didn't have any way of paying my bills and the whole mortgage. I guess I was pretty stupid about it though because I just kept writing cheques knowing they would bounce. Before I knew it I was £1000 overdrawn and horrid letters from the bank started raining down on me. I just wish I had told my bank what was going on earlier; perhaps I could have got a loan or something like that."
Grace (33)

(4) Don't borrow money off people you don't know or from adverts in the paper. The latter have extremely high interest rates and you could find yourself paying back the

loan twice over. The former is only a good idea if you are sure you can pay the money back soon. Many a good friendship has floundered over money.

"When I first became single I was so worried about not being able to pay my rent that I borrowed £500 off a close friend. Of course I couldn't pay it back and I found myself getting more and more upset every time I saw her. She never hassled me about it but it stayed between us for a long time. Even now I find it hard to look her in the eye without being embarrassed."
Sian (37)

3. Housing

One of the problems that arise when you become single again, if you have been living with your boyfriend, is accommodation. All fair and well if you live in your own house and have paid off your mortgage, but how many people have heavy mortgages hanging over their heads? And short of sleeping on a friend's sofa for the rest of your life, finding somewhere to live will be a priority. So take a look at your options:
(1) If you have been left with the house/flat: Work out if you can afford to stay there on your own. Take into account all the bills, rent/mortgage and what you have left possession-wise. If you think you can make it work, fine, but if you need help, now is the time to ask. Friends are brilliant at times like these and can supply you with any number of things, for example spare kettles, furniture, electrical goods, etc.
(2) You have nowhere to live: Most papers these days have a list of people who want room-mates and even the fussiest of people can find a room that fits their requirements. You could also go through a letting agency or estate agent but beware, most of them will charge you to find a room.

While you're looking, utilise your friends and family for contacts and places to stay.

(3) Can't afford the mortgage: First have a talk to the people who hold your mortgage. If you're behind on your payments see if you can pay them back over a number of months. If you are just worried about making the payments, why not rent out one of your rooms? Local colleges and universities always have students looking for rooms and an advert placed in the local paper can bring in a whole host of applicants. Also ask around; someone will know someone who is looking for a room.

Chapter 7

CHILDREN

There are a number of problems that arise when you become a single parent, but like everything they can be worked out.

1. Housing

Trying to find a place to live when you've got children is difficult but not impossible. There are a number of solutions to various problems. Firstly, you could always team up with another single parent and share a house between you. This is hard but as long as you work out what each of you wants, you'll end up with a happy solution.

"It was actually the TV show, Kate & Allie *that gave Karen and me the idea. I had just gone through a divorce and was looking for a place with my son who is 12. Karen owned a house and was having trouble paying the mortgage and she had a son as well. We have been friends for ages and decided to give it a try. It's worked really well for us and makes me feel like I am back in college again. I would never have been able to afford a house like this if I was by myself, so this is the perfect solution."*
Lucy (36)

2. Guilt

Trying to raise a family when you're part of a couple is hard enough, but on your own it feels nearly impossible. Apart from the practical worries of money and housing there is the added woe of feeling you're not giving them enough time or love.

"I look at my daughters and I continually feel guilty that I don't have enough time for them or enough money to give them what they want."
Pam (33)

"I always feel guilty because I spend my day rushing around trying to keep everything together for my kids and never quite manage it."
Jenni (28)

What you have to remember is, father or no father, the chances are you were probably this worried about your kids when you were part of a couple. Guilt is the silent booby prize no-one tells you about when you have children.

However, you can help yourself. Many councils run after-school groups for kids whose parents are working late and if you can't find them in your area, you could always try to set one up with other single parents in your area. It's no good complaining about lack of services if you aren't willing to do anything to help yourself. Also talk to your children. Let them know how you're feeling and more importantly let them know what's going on in your life. Shutting them out to protect them will bring a wall down between you.

"I think I was the last one to know that my mum and dad were splitting up and that really hurt because it felt like I wasn't important enough to tell."
Kelly (12)

"My mum works all day and at night when I try to talk to her she says she is too tired. I would like to see my father but I'm scared of upsetting her."
Stuart (14)

"I can hear my mum crying at night and when I ask her about it in the morning, she pretends she doesn't know what I am talking about. I feel she doesn't trust me enough to confide in me."
Anne (15)

"I felt really bad for my mum when she split up with her boyfriend because I liked him too. She felt like her life was over but when we talked about it, I think she realised that it wasn't the end of the world, and it wasn't, because now she's got another boyfriend who likes her as much as she likes him."
Linda (13)

3. Money Difficulties and Children

If you are really trying to get it together and it just isn't working, it may be time to ask for help. These days admitting you can't cope isn't taken as a sign of weakness by anyone. The age-old fear that the social services will jump on you and take your children away just isn't so any more. These days social services and community services are more likely to offer you competent help and advice to ease your situation and will also help you with housing difficulties. Other agencies that can help you in all manner of problems are listed at the end of the book.

4. Tips for Coping with Children as a Single Mother

(1) Talk to them. Let them know what's going on and why.
(2) Spend at least an hour a day with them.
(3) Ask them for their opinion.
(4) Get them to help you with the harder decisions.
(5) Admit to them that you are upset. Young people are not stupid, they can spot distress a mile off.
(6) Don't forget to tell them that just because you've split up and don't love each other any more doesn't mean that their father doesn't love them.
(7) Make certain that they know they weren't the cause of the break-up. They need a lot of reassurance on this – repeat it until you feel very satisfied that they understand.

(8) Listen to them. They can often come up with unexpected insights which you might find helpful.
(9) Get them to understand the positive aspects of having two households to visit.

Chapter Eight

"And in the end I realised that I took more than I gave.
I was trusted more than I trusted.
And I was loved more than I loved.
And what I was looking for,
was not to be found,
but to be made."
John Hughes

SOCIALISING

1. The Pain of Socialising

Heartbreak always seems like the pain to end all pain. You don't want to eat (or you don't want to stop eating), you sleep, you sit, you don't do anything but feel sad. And what's the last thing on your mind? Socialising, that's what. Yet socialising whether you want to or not is an important part of being single again. It's the only way you are ever going to realise that there is a life as a single person. A life that is fun and happy.

"Of course at first it was hard. I felt everyone was looking at me with pity. I had no desire to dress up or even get excited about anything. But after a couple of weeks I found myself looking forward to going for a drink with friends. And surprisingly, I even enjoyed it."
Beth (36)

Stay away from old haunts, they'll only bring those memories flooding back. Instead, think of new and exciting social events, things that sound crazy but fun, and rope your friends into doing things as well. Not only will you meet new people, but also, no-one need know that you're single again, which means no lengthy discussions on the break-up. The most important thing to remember when you're out supposedly enjoying yourself is that no-one is looking down on you in pity and no-one expects you to have a wonderful time whenever you step out of your front door. And while we're at it, drop those labels. Just because you are no longer someone's girlfriend/wife/lover, doesn't mean you automatically become a wallflower/spinster. Give yourself time and space and socialise at events that you want to go to, not that your friends want you to go to. Socialising is all about enjoyment and meeting people; don't let your misery blow it out of proportion and make every event into a trauma. Take each event at a time, and you'll soon find yourself enjoying life again.

2. Parties

Parties – does the very word strike fear into your heart? If it does, you're not alone. Parties are like company meetings. No-one really wants to go to them but you're annoyed if you don't get invited. Let's face it: what's fun about forcing yourself into an environment where the music blares so loud that the floorboards shake, people sweat until they smell, it's so dark that you can't see anyone you know and worse still, the only thing that's interested in you is the yucca in the corner? Or even worse, the drinks parties where people can't wait to find out what you do, who you're with and why you're by yourself.

3. Tips for Making Parties Bearable

(1) There is a way to enjoy parties, but first you have to decide why you're there in the first place. Is it because you want to meet someone? Is it because you've been bullied

into it? Or is it because you're in search of some elusive entertainment? If it's the first, stop right now. Men can spot a desperate woman a mile off and who knows who you'll end up with when broad daylight hits you. If it's the second, make the best of a bad situation and grin and bear it for as long as you can, then make a quick getaway.

(2) Make sure you know how you're going to get home. Having a boyfriend/husband makes little points like these a distant memory, but being single again it is important for two reasons. Firstly, no-one is responsible for your safety but you, and secondly, if you hate the party you need to know how you can escape. There's nothing worse than feeling miserable at a party all night, knowing that the girlfriend who's driven you there, intends to stay until 3 am and you've got no money to get away under your own steam.

(3) Don't over-drink. Easy enough to do when you're down. All that free drink and no-one to tell you to stop. But alcohol is a depressant and will make you feel even

worse. Also, it will put you in a fairly vulnerable position. Believe you me, being sozzled is a road to tears. While you're at it, think about that hangover you'll have tomorrow morning.

(4) Make sure you know at least three people there. You don't want to spend the whole night clinging to one person, do you? You'll feel bad and so will they. In any case the more people you know the more people you can be introduced to.

(5) If you're stuck for things to say, just take a deep breath and ask people questions about themselves. Being questioned, as long as it doesn't resemble the Spanish Inquisition, is really quite flattering. It will give you more to talk about, or less, depending on what you prefer.

(6) Arrive fashionably late. It will stop you feeling awkward about not knowing anyone and by the time you arrive the party will be in full swing.

(7) Make sure you wear something you feel great in. Going sloppily dressed or over-the-top sexy will only make you

feel as if you stick out like a sore thumb. Don't try to make a statement unless you're sure what you're trying to say.
(8) Don't go unless you like them. It's a popular myth that people love parties, but think about it – you wouldn't go to a football match unless you liked football – so don't go to parties if you hate them.

"I think parties are a complete and utter nightmare. Full of lovey-dovey couples and desperate singles. So I don't bother to go to them any more."
Pam (33)

"I love parties. You can really go fully out and enjoy them without any worry that you're going to make a fool of yourself."
Kelly (28)

"My best tip for parties is to take a group of friends with you. That way no matter what happens you've always got someone to dance with, talk with and have a good time with."
Joanne (40)

4. Christmas, Bank Holidays and Easter

Bank holidays and holidays are the scourge of the single life, the very days when being single hits home the hardest and hurts the most. There's something about the holiday season that makes people pair up, leave town or hibernate together, leaving us singles at a loose end, stuck watching Bank Holiday sport (great!) or attempting some DIY.

"I hate the holiday season. My parents live in Spain and all my friends are paired off. Holidays make me feel like a pathetic and miserable creature begging round for someone to take me in from the cold."
June (29)

But holidays don't have to be this way. If you take control of the situation you can make them work for you. The first thing you have to do is plan in advance. It's no good waiting till the last minute for something to be organised or asking people out. Most people look forward to holidays so much that they book themselves up weeks in advance. Start by planning something exciting. If you can afford it why not hire a house in the country and get all your friends to come down for the weekend. Or have a huge lunch for friends. Turn a day into a games extravaganza so children can come too. Or plan to go somewhere interesting.

"I love the holidays now. At first they were dreadful, the kids and I would just sit about and try to pretend we were having fun. Now I save up and make sure we go away in the holidays. Even if it's just for a couple of days, it's something to look forward to and something to enjoy."
Helen (35)

Helen is right, holidays are to be enjoyed, and if you haven't got a big family or one at all, it's up to you to make one out of friends and people you know. Most people are notorious for not wanting to organise their leisure time. They prefer someone else to do it for them. While this may seem like a pain, it is also a brilliant way of making sure you do something that you enjoy. No boring days fly fishing for you; instead, barbecues in the sun and video nights in the cold.

Of course, when you're unhappy it can be hard to immerse yourself in an activity or the excitement of the holiday season but if you try, your efforts will always pay off. Just make sure you involve other people in your plans. When you find your motivation flagging, it really helps to have someone to buck you up.

"My sister is great, she is always there encouraging me with

ideas for what I can do on the bank holidays. Even if she can't make it. She helps me think up trips I can take or parties I can have. It makes the whole holiday seem so much more fun."
Pam (29)

5. Travelling

For lots of women becoming single is a doorway to travelling and freedom. A time for themselves when they can do all the things they wanted to do without fear of upsetting someone else. In fact, more and more women are travelling alone these days, if not for business then definitely for pleasure.

"When I used to go on holiday with my boyfriend he would arrange everything, right from booking it, down to insurance. When he left me I had a choice for the summer; either I do it for myself or I stay in Britain for the summer. Finally I just did it. I couldn't believe how easy it was. Even the airport was as easy to deal with as the train station."
Clare (38)

"My husband would deal with the holidays all by himself. The only thing I had to do was make sure I was sitting next to him when the plane took off."
Katherine (32)

Going on holiday and/or travelling is actually a great way to broaden the mind. It teaches you to become self-confident, versatile, adventurous and to become the person you've always dreamed of being. It is probably the only time in life you'll completely get away from everyone who knows you. It's also a great way to forget a past relationship. If you are ready to take the plunge and want to travel alone for a number of months, then make sure you check everything out properly before you go. This

includes insurance, visas and work permits. Also check out your local bookshop for some guides for women travelling on their own.

"I decided to go off for a year when my relationship with Patrick ended. I was fed up with my life so I packed in my job and bought a round the world ticket. At first I was lonely but gradually I met lots of other women and men of all different ages and nationalities who were travelling on their own. And I had such fun going to places I had only previously dreamed of. Places like India, Africa, Australia. I think it's done me the world of good being able to see that I really can cope with life on my own. My God, if I can travel round India on my own I can cope in London on my own."
Janey (35)

Contrary to popular belief, holidaying alone doesn't have to mean anything like those "single" holiday tours. If you don't fancy doing it alone, there are alternatives. Many of the listings magazines around the country and especially the Sunday papers hold ads for trekking holidays for small groups or people who want someone to travel with. If this doesn't take your fancy you could always just book up with a package tour.

If you have children and can't afford to go away, there are a number of agencies you can contact for cheap holidays, details of which can be found through organisations for single parents listed at the end of this book. If you don't want to go abroad then why not book a house in the country with a group of friends? This is a good way to share the cost and also get away. Of course, prices vary between high and low season but sharing does reduce the cost. Airlines, holiday companies, and hotels all cater for children. This means if you fancy going out at night there will be someone who can look after your children and there will be cut-price deals for under-12s.

Another cheap holiday is to go and visit friends in a different town or country. A few pointers to watch out for here: don't expect them to entertain you all the time. Make sure you know what you want to do and make sure they don't run round after you. Also make sure you bring enough money and clothes and toiletries. After all, you're not staying in a hotel.

A final point is, let your friends and family know where you are going. Disappearing off the face of the earth for any amount of time is bound to have everyone fearing the worst. Just because you're single again doesn't mean no-one cares about you or worries about you. So leave a contact point with at least two friends and make sure you write some postcards. After all, you will be coming home one day so keep in touch with your friends.

6. Entertaining

Entertaining is a great way to socialise on your own terms. It means you can spend time with people who you really want to be with, do things that you want and all on home territory. Of course, it's fairly traumatic to have things like parties and dinners on your own, because you end up sinking or swimming without anyone to lean on. But then that's the thrill of it all.

"My first dinner party was so traumatic. My starter was a disaster, I burnt the chicken and worse still, I forgot to buy anything to drink. It was funny though because we all ended up laughing about it. It still comes up in conversation two years later."
Shauna (35)

If you're planning on having party here are a few tips to make sure it goes with a swing.
(1) Don't worry about people having a good time. If you leave them to their own resources they'll just get on with it and enjoy themselves.

(2) Make sure you have music available. There's nothing worse than silence.
(3) Invite all your very best friends; that way you'll have people to help and support you through the night.
(4) Designate a friend to keep the bottles open and help with the drinks, that will mean one less thing on your mind.
(5) Don't be afraid to ask people to bring a bottle to the party.

"My friends and I came up with a really good way of meeting new people when I became single again. One of us would throw a party and invite at least 15 people we knew well. Each of these 15 people would have to bring someone they knew but no-one else did. It worked wonderfully. It's been a long time since I've met so many new people."
Vicky (31)

"I used to hate entertaining when I was part of a couple. It always felt like too much effort. When I became single I realised that if I was going to have any social life whatsoever I had to make an effort and invite people round. Nowadays I quite enjoy it and actually look forward to doing it."
Emma (28)

Entertaining needn't mean a fancy dinner party or a huge party. It can be as simple as organising a picnic in the park, or a day out to the coast. So don't blow entertaining out of proportion. After all, you are meant to enjoy it. Make things as simple as possible for yourself. This means inviting the people you want, doing the things you like to do and not spoiling it with needless worry.

7. Dating Again: Do You Really Want a Boyfriend?

Are you one of those people who honestly feel that you can't live without a man in your life? Do you feel thoroughly incomplete when you haven't got a boyfriend? Are you always depressed and lonely on a Saturday night? If you're being honest, you've probably felt like this at least once in your life. It's a perfectly natural way to feel; pretty horrible I admit, but natural all the same. Part of the problem is that there is an awful lot of pressure for women to feel inferior and unattractive if they haven't got a man at their side.

If you're learning to survive on your own and not even thinking of dating again, then ignore this section. But for everyone else out there the first question you have to ask yourself is, Do you really want a boyfriend? And if the answer is yes, ask yourself why? Is it the intimacy you miss, the sex, having someone to share your life with or because you've met someone you really like?

Unfortunately, there is no magic cure for the sex and while some women find one-night stands and brief affairs solve their problems, the majority of women find little solace in them. The best advice is to discover what works best for you and live by that rule and no-one else's. Intimacy, however, can be a part of your life. Make sure you reach out to the people you love and tell them so once in a while. Even the most emotionally reticent of people respond when a friend reaches out to them. For instance, hug your friends when you see them. Tell them you appreciate them. Other people swear by pets, especially dogs and cats who love to be loved.

"The number of times I have been feeling down and unloved till my cat snuggled up to me. She makes me feel important and she's always there when I need someone to talk to at 2 am. She's the perfect solution when I need something to hug."
Mel (40)

If you want a boyfriend because you feel left out and empty then do realise that getting a man won't necessarily fulfil your life. You have to feel complete by yourself before you can feel complete with someone else. Remember, if you allow someone to become your reason for living you'll always run the risk of being completely devastated if he ever leaves.

What if you've met someone you really like? How do you begin to cope with the dating game again?

(1) To begin with, don't throw all your hard-learned lessons to the wind and just jump in the deep end. If you're asked out on a date, give yourself time to see if you like this new man.

(2) Realise that dating may be painful at first and you may keep remembering how dreadful you felt when your last relationship ended, but don't blame this man for your past relationships.

"When I first started dating, I found myself blaming my new boyfriend for all the misery I'd had in my marriage. I wouldn't trust him and didn't believe him when he said he loved me. In the end he said he couldn't take my insecurities any more and left. It's only now that I realise I wasn't ready to date then and I was only doing it because I'd been pushed into it by my friends."
Linda (35)

(3) If you don't want to date yet, then say so. There's nothing worse than letting your friends/family/work mates make you feel it's not okay to be single.

"I am very happy living the way I do, single and pretty much care-free. The trouble is my friends can't believe I am happy this way. They are all in relationships and can't believe people can be happy outside of one. The number of times they try to pair me up on blind dates. It drives me crazy."
Lisa (28)

(4) Don't latch on to someone new just because you're lonely. It's hard to stand your ground when you feel miserable but grabbing the first man who comes your way, won't make you feel any better.

"I've learnt my lesson now. Immediately after I divorced I'd go to clubs and pick up men thinking one of them would save me from my misery. None of them were interested in doing that, all they wanted was sex. Now I've met a really nice man and I think our relationship is working this time because I feel more ready for it. I'm not waiting to be saved any more."
Lara (34)

(5) Don't have sex until you feel ready. For some this will mean sooner rather than later, but never trade sex for affection because it won't work.
(6) There are plenty more fish in the sea. It really is important to realise that in time you'll meet someone new whom you'll like. The world is full of people and just because a relationship has failed doesn't mean you'll never have another one. People find love at all ages and at all times. So as the old song goes, "Never give up on a good thing. Remember, what makes you happy."

Chapter 9

LIVING HAPPILY EVER AFTER

"When you give up the longing for what might have been, you make room in your life for what can be and for the real people in your life – even if they're not perfect."
Bain & Sanders, *Out In The Open.*

In the fairytales of our childhood, stories always ended with handsome princes emerging from the forests and whisking any single fair maiden off into a life of supposedly happily married bliss. Real life, however, has a way of sometimes turning sour but thankfully, happily ever after doesn't just mean happiness with a man. Lots of women find that being single means happily ever after on their own.

From all the women interviewed for this book, many stories emerged of those who have triumphed from becoming single again. Some have successfully found new lives for themselves, others have brought up families on non-existent incomes and many many more have found that they really are stronger than they ever thought.

Being single again is more than living and being on your own. It's a chance to see what you really can achieve by yourself and for yourself. No-one is saying being single has to be for life but, remember, if you learn to cope successfully on your own you'll know nothing will ever be too much for you again.

CLARE, 24 years old:
"I had only been going out with David for two years which I know isn't very long and yet, I've always had a boyfriend since

I was 15, so when I became single again it was the first time I had ever been on my own.

"I am ashamed to admit it but I was always one of those girls who thought being single was somehow an embarrassment. I thought it showed that no-one liked you. It never even crossed my mind that some people do it out of choice. I hated being single again at first. I was lonely and bored all the time. I was also very angry at David for leaving me. My friends tried to be supportive but it's very annoying to have someone around who moans all the time about men.

"I don't know when I realised that I quite liked being on my own. I suddenly thought it was quite nice not to have to consult anyone when I wanted to go out. More importantly, being single has made me realise the importance of getting a life for myself. I've taken up night classes in French and I make more of an effort with my friends. After all, being single doesn't equal being lonely. I have a really nice, independent lifestyle and that's certainly something I don't regret."

SUE, 32 years old:
"Sometimes, I feel like I have been in and out of relationships all my life. I was never one of those girls happy to be single. I liked having a boyfriend because it made me feel important. Paul and I were together for six years and engaged for a further two years before we broke up.

"After we split, I became this pathetic wretch of a creature. Until you've been heartbroken you can't possibly understand how empty life feels when you're not with the person you love. Finally, I was fired from my job and that really put a different light on my life. I mean here I was, 30 years old, no job, no boyfriend and an empty life ahead of me.

"So I decided to travel. Leaving Britain was hard but exciting. I actually travelled for two years, working my way round the world. My friends say I have come back a completely different person, confident and happier than I've ever been in my life. This was more than a trip for me, I've decided to make

it my way of life. Now I've seen a bit of the world, I'm never going to stop trying to see more of it. I know my life-style horrifies some people but I can't enthuse about it enough. Sometimes, I wonder if I had married Paul what my life would have been like and that scares me more than trekking through jungles in South America."

ANNA, 38 years old:
"Breaking up is always hard to do even if you are the one who does it. Keith and I were married for 15 years and though it wasn't a terrible marriage it wasn't great either. Being single again has helped me to find out who my real friends are.

"I have never been the sort of person who thought they could do anything, but if you saw me now, fixing plugs and dealing with the everyday necessities of the house you'd think 'what a capable woman'. I still don't have a successful career, though I have started at night school which I love. I also go to the gym twice a week for aerobics with my daughter. It's great fun because there are people of all ages and sizes there. I don't see my husband much because he got remarried, but I do know that he is much happier than he was with me.

"I often think how funny it is that people fool themselves into thinking that they're happy when they're not. I think women are scared of being single again because other people make them feel it's not right. The thing is, when you deal with being single on a day-to-day basis it is actually easier than being in a relationship. I like the idea that sink or swim, you do it on your own. It's up to me now to make my life successful and there's something quite exciting and wonderful about that."

JOANNE, 40 years old:
"When my husband died I felt like it was the end of the world. I had always imagined us living together in old age, two people gardening and playing with our grandchildren. His death was even more devastating because it was so sudden. One minute he was there, the next he'd gone. The loneliness was the hardest thing to bear. Our three sons had already gone off to college so I'd gone from a noisy house to an empty one, a full life to an empty one.

"To begin with it was the companionship that I missed. I mean, we had been married for 22 years and it was terrible to be so alone. It's a good thing for me that I have such good

friends because without them I am sure I would have given up. They came and stayed with me when things got tough, helped me arrange the funeral and deal with life long after it was all over.

"I used to think that if my husband died it would be the worst thing that could ever happen to me and I was sure I would never get over it. I've learnt from his death that I'm stronger than I thought I was and that if I can cope with this I can cope with anything. These days, I look at life differently. I've learnt not to take things so seriously and that everything has a relatively funny side to it. This has made my life happier. I go out with friends and enjoy parties, days out and even holidays."

FINAL WORD:

LAUGHTER IS THE BEST MEDICINE

Laugh and the whole world laughs with you, cry and you cry alone. When things are bad it's always better to look on the funny side of things, if you can; after all, laughter is supposed to be the best medicine. One, it relieves the pressure of the situation, and two, it clears your brain and lightens your heart.

Laughter can actually help you deal with being single in a number of ways. Firstly it distracts you from pondering on the down side of being single. Then it reduces the anxiety you may feel about your new state of affairs; next, it makes the situation seem better; and then it increases the production of endorphins. Endorphins are tiny little nerve endings in the brain which, when released, make you feel happy. The same response is felt when you're in love, you eat chocolate (don't overdo this one) or have sex. They are actually the body's natural painkillers and responsible for making you feel better. If laughter causes us to release these endorphins and feel this pleasure, then what better excuse to laugh!

It is nearly always possible to view your situation in a different light and laugh at it. All it takes is a bit of initiative.

"The number of years I spent crying over my relationship, I can tell you – what a waste of time. These days I try to remember all the funny things or even better, all the terrible things. Like the time I found my boyfriend in bed with another girl. All I can remember now is thinking how unattractive he looked without his clothes on. It also makes me laugh to remember him running after me on the street with only my T-shirt wrapped round his waist."

Stephanie (27)

"The one thing I've learned in life is that the serious moments in my life haven't improved one bit just because I spoke seriously about them. So now I laugh."
Fiona (36)

"I used to go and watch my husband fish because he loved it. Every weekend, we'd set off at the crack of dawn to sit near some smelly river all day. I wasn't allowed to talk, but because I loved him, I convinced myself I was as interested in fishing as him. Of course I wasn't. Now I only have to see a fish and I crack up laughing. Sad, isn't it?"
Maggie (40)

USEFUL ADDRESSES

Smoking:
ASH (Action on Smoking and Health)
5–11 Mortimer Street
London W1N 7RH
Tel: 071 637 9843

Smoker's Quitline
102 Gloucester Place
London W1H 3DA
Tel: 071 487 3000

Drug Addiction:
Standing Conference on Drug Abuse (SCODA)
Kingsbury House
1–4 Hatton Place
Hatton Garden
London EC1N 8ND
Tel: 071 430 2341

Single Parents:
Gingerbread Association for One Parent Families
35 Wellington Street
London WC2E 7BN
Tel: 071 240 0953

National Council for One Parent Families
255 Kentish Town Road
London NW5 2LX
Tel: 071 267 1361

Housing:
Shelter
88 Old Street
London EC1V 9AX
Tel: 071 253 0202

Legal rights and benefits advice:
Citizens Advice Bureaux
136/144 City Road
London EC1V
Tel: 071 251 2000

Legal problems:
Law Centres Federation
Duchess House
Warren St
London W1P 5DA
Tel: 071 387 8570

Also in the series:

ARE YOU READY YET?
Preparing for a New Relationship
John Gordon
illustrated by Ray Jelliffe

When a relationship ends, through your own choice or not, it can take time to get over it. How do you know if you've really come to terms with the loss of your partner? Dare you put yourself in the vulnerable position of loving someone again? Do you really want another person in your life at the moment?

Here is a book which helps to negate the pain and sort out confused emotions. By making you feel safe and strong, you can decide whether you really are ready to begin a new relationship.